AMONG STRANGERS I'VE KNOWN ALL MY LIFE

PARMI LES ETRANGERS QUE J'AI CONNUS TOUTE MA VIE

Also by Sanford Fraser

14th Street
The New School Chapbook Series, 1995

Among Strangers I've Known All My Life/
Parmi Les Etrangers Que J'ai Connus Toute Ma Vie
Bilingual edition: Tarabuste Editions, 2007, France

Tourist
NYQ Books, 2009

AMONG STRANGERS I'VE KNOWN ALL MY LIFE

SANFORD FRASER

PARMI LES ETRANGERS QUE J'AI CONNUS TOUTE MA VIE
Traduction: Françoise Parouty

The New York Quarterly Foundation, Inc.
New York, New York

NYQ Books™ is an imprint of The New York Quarterly Foundation, Inc.

The New York Quarterly Foundation, Inc.
P. O. Box 2015
Old Chelsea Station
New York, NY 10113

www.nyqbooks.org

Copyright © 2010 by Sanford Fraser

All rights reserved. No part of this book may be used or reproduced in any manner whatsoever without written permission of the author. This book is a work of fiction. Any references to historical events, real people or real locales are used fictitiously. Other names, characters, places, and incidents are products of the author's imagination, and any resemblance to actual events or locales or persons, living or dead, is entirely coincidental.

NYQ Books is grateful to Tarabuste Editions, France for allowing us to present this United States edition of *Among Strangers I've Known All My Life/ Parmi Les Etrangers Que J'ai Connus Toute Ma Vie.*

First Edition

Set in New Baskerville

Layout by Raymond P. Hammond
Cover Design by Bob Cooley
Cover Photo: © 2010 Bob Cooley - www.bobcooleyphoto.com

Library of Congress Control Number: 2010934129

ISBN: 978-1-935520-33-7

For my parents
Pour mes parents

William Clayton and Helen Sanford Fraser

Acknowledgment

My grateful acknowledgment to the editors of the following journals in which poems appearing in this volume were published:

Ma gratitude aux éditeurs des journaux suivants où furent publiés des poèmes figurant dans ce volume:

In America:

Milkweed Anthology 2000
Mudfish
Parting Gifts
Poetic Justice
Stroker 66
The New York Quarterly
Turnstile
Wind

In France:

Arpa
Comme Ça Et Autrement
Décharge
Gros Textes
Phréatique
Triages

In Belgium:
Archipel
Microbe

I want to particularly thank Raymond Hammond, the Editor of NYQ Books, for his fine editing and for his patience and understanding. Also, I'm grateful to Françoise Parouty for her translations, to Bob Cooley for the cover, and to many friends for their suggestions, among them: Nancy Green, Jordan Cain, Pearl London, and Christian Garaud.

CONTENTS
TABLE DES MATIÈRES

Introduction / xi

IN THE LAND OF GRAVY
AU PAYS DE LA BOUFFE

In the Land of Gravy / 16
Au Pays de la Bouffe / 17
Sanitation / 18
Nettoyage / 19
Points of View / 20
Points de Vue / 21
Such a Nice Day / 22
Quelle Belle Journée / 23
Smoke / 24
Fumée / 25
Gulf / 26
Le Golfe / 27
Cellphone Man / 28
L'homme au Portable / 29
For Missing Prisoners of War / 30
Pour les Prisonniers de Guerre Portés Disparus / 31
Elevated / 32
Métro Aérien / 33
Amtrak Limited / 34
Dans le Train / 35
Number 4 / 36
Le Quatrième / 37
Everything's a Sign / 38
Toute Chose est un Signe / 39
TV Dinner / 40
Plateau-Télé / 41
Isabel Weeds / 42
Isabelle Désherbe / 43
Neighbor / 44
Voisinage / 45
Getting Ready / 46
Prêt à Partir / 47

Crossing   / 48
En Traversant   / 49
Tourist   / 50
Touriste   / 51

UNDERGROUND STATION
STATION SOUTERRAINE

Underground Station   / 54
Station Souterraine   / 55
Be Cool   / 56
Sois Cool   / 57
Friday Night   / 58
Vendredi Soir   / 59
Spiders   / 60
Les Araignées   / 61
Macho   / 62
Macho   / 63
Beautiful   / 64
Ma Belle   / 65
Ode to a Waitress   / 66
Ode à la Serveuse   / 67
Hanging Out   / 68
L'Ecole Buissonière   / 69
Blond   / 70
Blonde   / 71
My Passionate Part   / 72
Mon Rôle Passionné   / 73
Of Course There's Someone Else   / 74
Bien Sûr il y a Quelqu'un d'Autre   / 75
Circe   / 76
Circé   / 77
In My Garden   / 78
Dans Mon Jardin   / 79
O Susan Hot Sauce   / 80
O Suzanne Sauce Piquante   / 81

SOMEWHERE YOUNG AGAIN
JEUNE A NOUVEAU

Somewhere Young Again   / 84
Jeune à Nouveau   / 85
The Ticking   / 86
Tic-Tac   / 87
Open Window   / 88
Fenêtre Ouverte   / 89
Elevator   / 90
L'Ascenseur   / 91
Looking Out to Sea on the Uptown Express   / 92
La Mer Revue à Bord du Métro Nord Express   / 93
Fishes   / 94
Les Poissons   / 95
Sometimes in his Poem   / 96
Quelquefois dans son Poème   / 97
The Happy Hour   / 98
Happy Hour   / 99
Undergrowth   / 100
Sous Bois   / 101
Here? At the A & P   / 102
Ici? Au Supermarché   / 103

INTRODUCTION

Sanford Fraser, whom I have had the great good fortune & privilege to know for nearly two decades, is a poet's poet, and largely unheard of outside a small circle of discerning readers and friends. If this bilingual edition of *Among Strangers I've Known All My Life* brings him a wider audience, it will be an important literary event.

Fraser was born in Boston in 1932. He began writing poetry at the age of fifty in New York where he now lives. He has been a student of painting in Paris and a social worker in New York. He has a degree in literature from Wesleyan University and a Ph.D. degree in art education from New York University. He has been published in leading poetry magazines in America & Europe.

In the tradition of Robert Lowell and Emily Dickinson, Fraser is a New England poet. His are small precise images, giant leaps of imagination, and he makes perfect word choices, most especially in his unpretentious verbs that lead him to an exploration of an inner life of deep existential loneliness, a thoroughgoing isolation with fleeting flashes of connection with others.

He is also a New York City poet, like Gregory Corso and Frank O'Hara. He is endlessly fascinated with the hidden meanings of life lived in an urban environment, in restaurants, on the street, on buses, on crowded sidewalks, in the subway. The natural world is for him mysterious, a pigeon in an airshaft, love a memory, interactions with other humans dangerous and tentative.

In addition, he is a bold, bohemian experimenter, like Boston's Bill Knott, not nearly as well known as he should be, even among his fellow American poets. Yet those who do have the privilege of knowing his work follow closely his output of masterpieces, on occasion jealous of the clarity, resonance, and seeming simplicity of his spare lines.

Each poem (typically 4-16 lines) is a Russian novel, a miniature painting, a movie script, a complete memoir, a nuanced biography, a disturbing newspaper clipping. Within all this complexity is a straightforward aesthetic. "Most of my poems are short. The narrator or speaker is usually a character in the poem, talking to himself or to someone else."

Let two of his poems speak for themselves.

The first is "My Wall."

> *My wall is always here*
> *invisible in front of me.*
> *I feel safe behind it*
> *protected*
> *and of course*
> *locked up.*
> *You're somewhere out there*
> *behind your own wall.*
> *Often, our walls stand together*
> *talk at each other*
> *their words bouncing*
> *back & forth*
> *not saying much*
> *just having a nice time.*

The second he calls "The Snowman."

> *All day*
> *the snow falling*
> *going nowhere:*
> *I grow fat*
> *my footprints*
> *like soft words*
> *disappear*
> *into the white street.*
> *Frozen inside myself*
> *I feel nothing*
> *my thoughts pile up*
> *and drift away.*

Some have it that the poet writes one long poem. The poems of Sanford Fraser are positive proof that our very best poets do in fact refine over time a small number of themes and treatments until they contain everything known & felt to be true, everything that needs to be passed on through language, sound, and vision to the future, if the future is even a little interested.

Angelo Verga
New York City, July 26, 2010

Angelo Verga is the author of six collections of poetry, the most recent being *Praise for What Remains,* Three Rooms Press, 2009. Widely published & translated, he resides in lower Manhattan.

In the Land of Gravy

Au Pays de la Bouffe

There's no strutting we do
Like my neighbor's pigeons who've brought down
Some straw of snatched-up sunlight in their beaks....

Ici on ne se pavane pas
comme les pigeons du voisin
apportant dans leur bec une paille de soleil volé....

—Jean Garrigue

In The Land of Gravy

A new Caddy floats
on my mashed potatoes
blue chip stocks copulate
in my bowl of pea soup
bubbling blondes pop up
in my Cabernet Sauvignon.

My paunch fills
like a hot-air balloon
and still I consume
I consume.

Au Pays de la Bouffe

Une Cadillac neuve flotte
dans ma purée
des actions en or s'accouplent
dans mon potage
des blondes effervescentes nagent
dans mon Cabernet Sauvignon.

Mon estomac s'emplit
tel une montgolfière
et je consomme encore
je consomme.

Sanitation

I see the mammoth truck
scraping garbage
into its gut:
heels of rye bread
inside a torn sweater,
burnt steak and fries
bleeding ketchup,
stripped corncob
covered by the Times.

Beside my bed
iron tusks appear
and scrape my chest.

I don't complain
it's just another cleanup.
I pull myself together
slowly rise into the noise
drink some coffee
listen to the news:

Djarkarta Riot Broken
Market Gains
Low Pressure Moving In.

Nettoyage

Je vois l'énorme camion
engloutissant les restes
comme un mammouth :
des quignons de pain
dans un chandail déchiré,
un steak-frites brûlé
saignant de ketchup,
un épi de maïs grignoté
recouvert de journaux.

Au pied de mon lit
des défenses en fer apparaissent
me transpercent la poitrine.

Je ne me plains pas
ce n'est qu'un autre nettoyage.
Je reprends mes esprits
me lève lentement dans le vacarme
bois du café
en écoutant les nouvelles :

L'émeute est brisée à Djakarta
La Bourse est en hausse
L'orage approche.

Points of View

On rooftops in Chokwe people watch
dark clouds approach.

A food expert in New York says
"Be sure to plan each meal in advance."

Water fills the African Village:
the fields become lakes.

"Fish, nuts, and Basmati rice
are good for you."

A helicopter lifts an old woman
through the air.

"Small portions of dessert
permissible."

Bloated cows float by.
Bone-thin children stare.

Points de Vue

Sur les toits de Chokwe les gens regardent
s'approcher de sombres nuages.

A New York un expert en nutrition déclare :
« Soyez sûr de prévoir chaque repas à l'avance. »

L'eau envahit le Village Africain:
les champs deviennent des lacs.

« Le poisson, les noix et le riz Basmati
sont excellents pour la santé. »

Un hélicoptère emporte une vieille femme
dans les airs.

« Petites portions de dessert
autorisées. »

Des vaches enflées flottent.
Des enfants squelettiques me dévisagent.

Such a Nice Day

The air-conditioner trudging
(as if going somewhere)
neighbors walking their dogs
the morning waking up
an old man coughing.

Such a nice day
another war
another shooting
children on their way to school
young men in green fatigues
their rifles shining.

Such a nice day
scrambled eggs
and coffee
clumps of grass patching the yard
the sprinkler working
a game at one.

Quelle Belle Journée

La clime s'essouffle
(comme si elle allait quelque part)
des voisins promènent leurs chiens
le matin se lève
un vieillard tousse.

Quelle belle journée!
encore une guerre
encore un massacre aux actualités
des enfants sur le chemin de l'école
des jeunes gens en treillis
leurs fusils luisants.

Quelle belle journée!
deux œufs brouillés
et du café
des touffes d'herbe rapiècent le jardin
l'arrosoir est en marche
un match à une heure.

Smoke?

Voices in the hall
are asking questions.

I type faster.
I don't want to hear them.

Suddenly fire engines race
through my mind.

My words stop.
I wait for the sound of sirens in the street

for the blue sky
to crash.

Fumée ?

Les voix dans le couloir
posent des questions.

Je tape plus vite.
Je ne veux pas les entendre.

Tout à coup, d'énormes camions rouges
font la course dans ma tête.

Mes mots s'arrêtent.
J'attends les sirènes dans la rue.

J'attends que le ciel bleu
s'effondre.

The Gulf

> for Jalel El Gharbi

In my son's hand
a model jet
dives
plastic wings
over enemies
on our front lawn.

On TV the General talks
in camouflage.
No one sees the bomber
overhead.
During the ad for Ivory Snow
blood and oil seep through the screen.

Le Golfe

    à Jalel El Gharbi

Dans la main de mon fils
un jet miniature
plonge
des ailes en plastique
vers les ennemis
sur notre pelouse.

Le Général parle à la télé
en camouflage.
Personne ne voit le bombardier
au-dessus des têtes.
Pendant la publicité pour une lessive
du sang et du pétrole filtrent
à travers l'écran.

Cellphone Man

Coming toward me
his eyes look
long distance

not at me
not at the street
thick with traffic.

He's pressing buttons
probably phoning his office.
He's hogging the walk.

I jump.
Even the pigeons hop
out of his way.

L'homme au Portable

Il se dirige vers moi
ses yeux regardent
au loin

non pas sur moi
ni sur la rue
encombrée par le trafic.

Il appuie sur des touches.
Nul doute il appelle son bureau.
Il accapare le trottoir.

Je m'écarte.
Même les pigeons s'envolent
sur son passage

For Missing Prisoners of War

Bikers in black leather
circle the Battery this Sunday afternoon
their bodies rigid, their knees spread high.

They don't look at the tourists
lined-up for the short trip
to Ellis Island or to the Statue of Liberty.

Small American flags
hang from their rear wheels.
The bursts of their engines

ricochet
off empty Wall Street buildings.

Pour les Prissoniers de Guerre Portés Disparus

Des motards en cuir noir font le tour
du Parc de la Batterie ce dimanche après-midi
le corps raide, les genoux hauts.

Ces vétérans ne regardent pas les touristes
alignés pour le court voyage
à Ellis Island ou à La Statue de la Liberté.

De petits drapeaux américains
pendent de leurs roues arrières.
Le vacarme de leurs moteurs

ricoche
sur les immeubles vides de Wall Street.

Elevated

Above the honking street
the train lifts me
in my gray suit.

Below the track
a biker zooms
through traffic.

My hand twists the throttle.
My elbows cock
like wings in leather.

Métro Aérien

Au-dessus de la rue hurlante
le train me soulève
dans mon costume gris.

Sous les voies
une moto fonce
à travers le trafic.

Ma main agrippe la poignée.
Mes coudes s'incurvent
telles des ailes de cuir.

Amtrak Limited

Across the aisle you sit
stiff and still
a manikin in tweed.

A current Vogue hogs the place by your side.
Ads from today's Times barricade your face
and usher you to condos high on suburb hills:

the crew cut tennis court and blue-eyed pool
the flannel men and cashmere girls
in Coppertone skin and custom-made curls…

At Mystic Harbor the masts of vacant yachts wink
outside your window.
Boarding passengers pause, glance at you

move on.

Dans le train

Vous êtes assise en face
raide et muette
un mannequin de tweed.

Un numéro de Vogue occupe le siège à côté de vous.
Les annonces du Times bloquent votre visage
et vous emmènent dans les résidences
des beaux quartiers de banlieues:

le court de tennis coupé en brosse, la piscine aux yeux bleus
les hommes en flanelle, les filles en cachemire
au teint bronzé et à la coiffure ondulée…

au Mystic Harbor, les mâts des yachts vides
clignent de l'œil à la fenêtre.
Les voyageurs s'arrêtent, vous regardent

passer.

Number 4

…and Julia's husband, you've heard?
Dead near the Bleecker café where I lost my purse
Manhattan toppling over in his eyes without warning
on the way to his car.

He's number 4 in my building this year.
I'm sure you know him well
a quiet man
the flag sewn on his shoulder.

And Julia, what's her last name?
I must send a note.

Le Quatrième

…et pour le mari de Julia, vous avez entendu?
Mort près du café Bleecker là où j'ai perdu mon sac
Manhattan qui s'écroule dans son regard
sans prévenir, se dirigeant vers sa voiture.

C'est le quatrième dans mon immeuble cette année.
Je suis sûre que vous le connaissiez
un homme tranquille
un drapeau cousu sur son col.

Et Julia? J'ai oublié son nom de famille.
Il faudra que j'envoie un mot.

Everything's a Sign

Of everything else:
the morning waking up,
an old man coughing.
My neighbors, actors:
some walking dogs
others, jogging.

The voices I hear
the faces I see
all commercials on TV.

Such a nice day.
Did I say that? did you?
Words like ice cream cones
in soft white paper napkins
completely shock-and-moisture proof

words from 9 to 5
in suits that never say anything
not said before.

Tout chose est un Signe

De toute autre chose:
le matin qui se réveille,
un vieillard qui tousse.
Mes voisins, des acteurs:
certains, promènent des chiens
d'autres, font du jogging.

Les voix que j'entends
les visages que je vois
des pubs à la télé.

Quelle belle journée.
J'ai dit cela? Et toi tu l'as dit?
Des mots comme des cornets de glace
dans des serviettes en papier douces et blanches
complètement à l'épreuve du choc et de l'humidité

des mots de 9 à 5
abillés en complets qui ne disent rien
que du déjà dit.

TV Dinner

From my easy chair
I view & chew

miles of film:
lush bodies

in gourmet sets
shot close-up:

filtered actors
in living color,

hugging & mugging
killing & kissing.

Plateau-Télé

De mon fauteuil rembourré
je regarde et je mâche

des kilomètres de film :
des corps voluptueux

dans des scènes gourmandes
tournées en gros plan :

des acteurs filtrés
en couleur vivante,

qui s'enlacent et s'agressent
se tuent et s'embrassent.

Isabel Weeds

In Isabel's living room
the mantel clock chimes at no one
through its brass-rimmed face.
The fat sofa cushions
(wrapped in thick plastic)
sit alone
like the meat in a supermarket tray.

In the backyard, a summer night
falls into long, collapsible chairs.
Isabel leans on her crutches, hunting
the weeds in her husband Harry's new-cut grass:
"Here's a little rascal, dear," she says
(holding the weed up for proof)
"I found another one."

Harry murmurs, "Yes hon," from his hammock sling
and dreams her young and fair
a dead cigar in his smile—
"Looks like rain," he adds.

At ten, the fireflies start to spark
(even the moon begins to blush).
Isabel frowns at Harry's lit cigar
and swings on wooden wings around the house
to dust the plants and scold the dog.

Isabelle Désherbe

Dans le salon d'Isabelle
la pendule au cadran de cuivre
ne sonne plus pour personne.
Les gros coussins du sofa
(recouverts d'un plastique épais)
sont assis tout seuls comme
de la viande au rayon du supermarché.

Dans le jardin, une nuit d'été
tombe sur des chaises longues.
Isabelle, s'appuie sur ses béquilles,
chasse les mauvaises herbes de la pelouse
fraîchement tondue par son mari Harry.
«Encore une petite coquine, chéri», dit-elle
 (brandissant l'herbe comme preuve)
«J'en ai trouvé une autre.»

De son hamac, Harry murmure, «Oui, chérie»
et l'imagine, jeune et belle
un cigare éteint á la bouche.
Il ajoute: «On dirait qu'il va pleuvoir».

À dix heures, les lucioles commencent à briller
(même la lune se met à rougir).
Isabelle grimace au cigare qu'Harry fume
et sur ses ailes de bois s'envole dans la maison
pour épousseter les plantes et gronder le chien.

Neighbor

I always speak first.
Sometimes you answer

as though being forced by me
to let a word, a tiny hello

drop from your mouth
to the sidewalk.

Today you seem invincible
you have reinforcements:

you're laughing with friends
on the stoop next door

and standing in the crutches
you sometimes wear.

I put on my friendly smile
raise my hand to wave.

You look at me
then quickly turn away.

I stumble home
someone else.

Voisinage

Je parle toujours le premier.
Parfois vous répondez

comme si vous étiez obligé
de laisser un mot, un petit bonjour

tomber de votre bouche
sur le trottoir.

Aujourd'hui vous semblez invincible
vous avez des renforts :

vous riez avec des amis
sur le perron d'à côté

debout sur les béquilles
que vous utilisez quelquefois.

J'arbore un sourire amical
fais un signe de la main.

Vous me regardez et vite
vous vous détournez.

Je rentre en chancelant,
comme quelqu'un d'autre.

Getting Ready

My mind flies out
of here

dives
down flights of stairs

glides
to the stoop

to the pigeon
standing there yesterday

on one foot
its wings vibrating

about to take off.

Prêt à Partir

Mon esprit s'envole
hors d'ici

plonge
dans les escaliers

glisse
jusqu'au perron

jusqu'au pigeon
qui s'y tenait hier

sur une patte
vibrant des ailes

prêt à décoller.

Crossing

I must cross before the light changes
the sign's flashing DONT WALK DONT WALK.

That long white limo's inching forward.
An old man I bet behind the dark window

probably poking the floor with his damn cane
telling the driver DRIVE ON DRIVE ON.

Or maybe he's young like this stud on the Harley
cocking his elbows in leather and brass.

Gunning, gunning his engine.
I'M CROSSING I'M CROSSING.

En Traversant

Il faut que je traverse avant que le feu change :
le signal clignote DONT WALK DONT WALK.

Une longue limousine blanche gagne des centimètres.
Un vieillard je suppose derrière la vitre fumée.

Il frappe sûrement le sol de sa maudite canne
en disant au chauffeur ALLEZ ALLEZ.

Ou peut-être est-il jeune comme l'étalon sur sa Harley,
renflant ses épaules de cuir et de métal.

Il emballe, emballe son engin.
JE TRAVERSE JE TRAVERSE.

Tourist

My head,
prayer-bent over a folded map

my eyes, walking
lines

of streets
I don't have time to see

I look up
somewhere lost

among
strangers

I've known
all my life.

Touriste

Ma tête, inclinée comme en prière
sur une carte pliée

mes yeux marchant
le long

des rues
que je n'ai pas le temps de voir

je lève les yeux
perdu quelque part

parmi
des étrangers

que j'ai connus
toute ma vie.

Underground Station

Station Souterraine

Underground Station

Below the summer street
of sleeveless shirts
and baseball caps
of cellphones ringing

below the orange, red,
and purple hair
of tattooed boys & girls
on skateboards surfing

the bolted columns stand
like trunks of steel trees
against the rumbling wind
of passing trains.

Station Souterraine

Sous la rue estivale
des chemises sans manches
des casquettes de base-ball
et des portables qui sonnent

sous les cheveux oranges
rouges et violets
des garçons et des filles tatoués
surfant sur des planches

les colonnes boulonnées se dressent
telles des troncs d'arbres d'acier
contre le grondement du vent
des trains qui passent.

Be Cool

Put on baggy, long jeans
and a T-shirt

pierce your ears and nose
your lips and tongue

hide your eyes
in dark glasses

hang a blue tattoo
around your neck like a chain.

Now, saunter toward me
with your shoulders rocking.

Pretend
I'm not here.

Sois Cool

Mets tes jeans bouffants
et un T-shirt

perce tes oreilles
tes lèvres et ta langue

cache tes yeux
derrière tes lunettes noires

pends un tatouage à ton cou
en guise de chaîne.

Puis, pavane-toi pour moi
en balançant les épaules.

Fais comme si
je n'étais pas là.

Friday Night

From across the street
loud, drunken curses

hidden beneath trees
break into my room

and hover
over my bed.

I want to reach up
and grab them

throw them
back.

Long after they leave
I repeat them to myself.

Unseen and detached
they loiter

on a dark corner
of my mind.

Later, I wake up
shouting them.

Vendredi soir

De l'autre côté de la rue
des jurons ivrognes et braillards

cachés sous les arbres
pénètrent dans ma chambre

et planent
au-dessus de mon lit.

Je veux me lever
les attraper

et les renvoyer.

Longtemps après leur départ
je me les répète.

Sans être vus et détachés
ils rôdent

dans un coin sombre
de mon esprit.

Plus tard, je me réveille
en les hurlant.

Spiders

From tunnels & subways
on weekend nights they come
crisscrossing the street
from bar to bar.

In black leather
some lean against cars
others straddle bikes
their engines revving.

Long lines of them
block the sidewalk
with boomboxes
bursting.

One of them always strays
below my window.
Slowly, the invisible thread
of my thought binds him.

Without looking
down
I step on his back
and hear it crack.

Les Araignées

Des tunnels et des métros
en fin de semaine
ils sortent la nuit
zigzaguent de bar en bar.

En cuir noir
certains adossés à des voitures
d'autres chevauchent des bécanes
moteurs en marche.

De longues queues
bloquent le trottoir
leurs radios
à plein tube.

L'un d'eux s'égare toujours
sous ma fenêtre.
Lentement, le fil invisible
de ma pensée l'attache.

Sans regarder
en bas
je marche sur son dos
et l'entends craquer.

Macho

I see his face
everywhere:

on TV
in the street

a wooden face
that's like a wall

without windows
the eyes turned

inward
stalking

me.

Sometimes I want
to be him:

wear a new T-Shirt
carefully torn

use the latest drug
drive a Harley

turn on
a leather girl

fit her to me
like a glove.

Macho

Je vois son visage
partout

à la télé
dans la rue

son visage de bois
comme un mur

sans fenêtres
les yeux tournés

vers l'intérieur
me suivant.

Quelquefois je veux
être lui :

porter un tee-shirt neuf
soigneusement déchiré

prendre la drogue en vogue
conduire une Harley

allumer
une fille en cuir

la mettre sur moi
comme un gant.

Beautiful

Come over here
he whispers

from his
sidewalk table.

Come over here.
Now.

His eyes travel
up & down her body.

She says nothing
looks straight ahead

and keeps walking.

He snaps her
into his instant camera.

You're over here now.

Ma Belle

Viens ici
chuchote-t-il

de sa table
en terrasse.

Viens ici.
Tout de suite.

Ses yeux parcourent
son corps de haut en bas.

Elle ne dit rien
regarde tout droit

et continue de marcher.

Il la prend
avec son appareil photo.

Tu es ici maintenant.

Ode to a Waitress

What do you want?
she casually asked the air
above my head

You.
I want you
I said to myself.

A corn muffin and coffee
please.

The muffin toasted?
No, just plain
and cold.

Ode à la Serveuse

Qu'est-ce que vous voulez ?
demande-t-elle distraitement
par-dessus ma tête.

Toi.
C'est toi que je veux
pensais-je.

Un muffin et du café
s'il vous plaît.

Le muffin grillé?
Non, simple
et froid.

Hanging Out

The three of us
drinking Pepsi

Jenny leaning
against the counter

Roger next to her
his hand sliding up &

down her arm
as if he were stroking

a dog
absent-mindedly.

No words
spoken

his eyes saying
Watch me.

L'Ecole Buissonnière

Nous trois
buvant du Pepsi

Jenny accoudée
au comptoir

Roger à côté d'elle,
de la main lui frôle

le bras
comme s'il caressait

un chien
distraitement.

Sans dire
un mot

ses yeux me disent
regarde-moi.

Blond

I climb the long flight of stairs.
Hope my chair's free.

Few persons in the reading room today.
She's sitting at my table.

I feel the hard wood beneath my fingers.
She's resting her head on her arm.

I open my book.
Blonde hair fills each page.

Blonde

Je monte le grand escalier.
J'espère que ma place est libre.

Peu de gens dans la salle de lecture aujourd'hui.
Elle est assise à ma table.

Je sens le bois dur sous mes doigts.
Elle pose la tête sur son bras.

J'ouvre mon livre.
Des cheveux blonds à chaque page.

My Passionate Part

You come to bed like a sleepwalker
looking for someone else.
I pretend not to notice.
"Can I do something?"
My hands touch you.
You push them away.

Smaller and smaller I grow
till I'm your polite little man.
You're the soft pink blanket
I hug and put in my mouth.
Before I sleep
my fat and tiny fingers touch your smile.

Mon Rôle Passionné

Tu viens te coucher comme une somnambule
qui cherche quelqu'un d'autre.
Je fais semblant de ne rien voir.
«Est-ce que je peux faire quelque chose pour toi?»
Mes mains te frôlent.
Tu les repousses.

Je deviens de plus en plus petit
jusqu'à n'être que ton gentil petit homme.
Tu es la douce couverture rose
que je serre et mets dans ma bouche.
Avant de m'endormir
mes petits doigts boudinés frôlent ton sourire.

Of Course There's Someone Else

The building where you live
whispers "fuck you" when I walk by.
The whole block talks
behind my back.

He's with you now, stroking your arm.
You're telling him about me,
smiling your little smile
he understands so well.

Of course my paintings still hang
on your wall.
You can't get rid of them.
You can't get rid of me.

"You keep them?" he smirks.
You keep them all.

Bien Sûr il y a Quelqu'un d'Autre

l'immeuble où tu habites
me dit «MERDE» quand je passe.
Tout le pâté de maisons
bavarde dans mon dos.

Il est avec toi maintenant, te caresse le bras.
Tu lui parles de moi,
souriant de ton petit sourire
qu'il comprend si bien.

Bien sûr mes tableaux sont toujours là
sur ton mur.
Tu ne peux pas t'en défaire.
Tu ne peux pas te défaire de moi.

«Tu les gardes?» dit-il en grimaçant.
Tu les gardes tous.

Circe

Sexy babe
Movie star

I make you up
with the glossy parts

of cover girls I cut
from old magazines.

I'm your pig,
your giant snout.

I squeal & grunt
sniffing scraps of you all day.

In my fantasy at night
I'm your king, your master, your monster.

You're the lovely body
I paste together

and flip
away.

Circé

Nana sexy,
star de cinéma,

je te fabrique
avec des morceaux

de cover-girls que je découpe
de vieux magazines.

Je suis ton cochon
ton museau géant

qui couine et grogne
en reniflant tes restes toute la journée.

Dans mes fantasmes chaque nuit
je suis ton roi, ton maître, ton monstre.

Tu es le corps luisant
que j'assemble

et jette
en l'air.

In My Garden

> …il faut cultiver notre jardin.
> Voltaire

In my garden
I'm always shaved
and fully dressed
the tree always trimmed
the hedge clipped

each flower labeled
with its Latin name
a Bachelor's Button
(Centaurea Cyanus)
in my lapel

everything fixed
on display
laughter and children
strictly forbidden.

Where's Love? you ask.
Next to me
in the white evening gown
the mannequin

immaculate
and thin.

Dans Mon Jardin

>...il faut cultiver notre jardin.
>Voltaire

Dans mon jardin
je suis toujours rasé
et bien habillé
l'arbre toujours coupé
la haie bien taillée

chaque fleur étiquetée
avec son nom latin
un bouton de célibataire
(Centaurea Cyanus)
à la boutonnière

tout est organisé
comme une vitrine
le rire et les enfants
formellement interdits.

Et l'Amour? direz-vous.
À côté de moi
en robe du soir blanche
un mannequin

mince et
immaculé.

O Susan Hot Sauce

O Susan Hot Sauce
cold noodle girl
dumpling spare rib
hot spring roll

O take-out bucket
wonton sweet and sour
paradise chicken
spiced lotus flower

O snow-pea-baby-shrimp-cup of tea
ice cream cookie
come back to me.

O Suzanne Sauce Piquante

O Suzanne Sauce Piquante
vierge des nouilles froides
beignet côtelette
rouleau de printemps chaud

O paquet à emporter
wonton doux amer
poulet de paradis
fleur de lotus sucrée

O petit pois, bébé crevette, tasse de thé
gâteau glacé
reviens à moi.

Somewhere Young Again

Jeune à Nouveau

Somewhere Young Again

Halfway up the hill
the house remains
its walls, a giant hull
beside the tar road,
the distant sea, flat and still
like the blue in one of your oils.

Dreaming behind a thread
of cigarette smoke
you rest on the veranda.
Are you with a friend
somewhere young again?
The bright sun won't tell.

In an old photograph
you lean against a rowboat
near the water's rough edge.
Do you feel the house gently rising
its windows no longer shaking
endless waves coming in?

Jeune à Nouveau

La maison se tient toujours
au milieu de la colline
ses murs, une coque géante
au bord de la route goudronnée,
la mer au loin, calme et plate
comme le bleu dans une de tes toiles.

Rêvant derrière un filet
de fumée de cigarette
tu es assise sous la véranda.
Es-tu avec un ami
jeune à nouveau ?
Le soleil éclatant n'en dit rien.

Sur une vieille photo
tu t'appuies sur une barque
au bord d'une mer agitée.
Sens-tu la maison s'envoler doucement ?
Les fenêtres ne claquent plus
d'éternelles vagues y pénètrent.

Ticking

I didn't notice it
until the dark silence
let it in.

Now that's all I hear:
the alarm clock
beating inside me.

I can't stop it.
Sometime
(I don't know when)

it will go off.

Tic-Tac

Je ne l'avais pas remarqué
avant que l'obscur silence
le laisse entrer.

Maintenant je n'entends plus que lui :
le réveil
qui bat en moi.

Je ne peux pas l'arrêter.
Parfois
(je ne sais pas quand)

il va sonner.

Open Window

The long whisper of distant traffic
like the sound of surf
from the round wall of the sea
on wet sand rising,
the full sky sailing
in its clouds,
the hushed street
in footsteps

through this room of cups & pills
the curtain billowing

Fenêtre Ouverte

Le long soupir des voitures lointaines
tel le bruit des vagues
de la muraille marine
qui se lève sur le sable mouillé,
le ciel lourd navigant
dans ses nuages,
la rue amortie
sous ses pas

à travers cette chambre de fioles et de pilules
le rideau qui se gonfle

Elevator

Passing my floor
the elevator rises higher & higher.

I see Death in her gray uniform.

She says nothing to me.
I pretend She's not there:

I'm five years old
we're on a roller coaster

climbing higher & higher
about to fall.

I brace myself:
The elevator begins to wobble.

She stands by the door
waiting.

L'Ascenseur

Passant mon étage
l'ascenseur va de plus en plus haut.

Je vois la Mort en uniforme gris.

Elle ne me dit mot.
Je prétend qu'elle n'est pas là.

J'ai cinq ans.
On est sur le Grand Huit.

On monte de plus en plus haut
jusqu'à tomber.

Je me raidis :
l'ascenseur vibre.

Elle se tient à la porte.
Elle attend.

Looking Out to Sea on the Uptown Express

Between pale office workers
in button-down collars
on the rush-hour car,
a tanned girl in sweater
and shorts ponders
giant blue graffiti waves pound-
ing the exit door.

Cresting whitecaps break
over her
hot sand travels the rock-
ing floor
a gull begins to shriek.

The train stops.

Small round white stones skip-
ping up the aisle
pause
to tease her toes.

La Mer Revue à Bord du Métro Nord Express

Entre de pâles employés de bureau
en col de chemise boutonné
dans le wagon aux heures de pointe,
une fille bronzée en pull-over et short
contemple
d'immenses vagues de graffiti bleus
se brisant contre la portière.

Des crêtes d'écume blanche
roulent sur elle
du sable chaud glisse
sur le sol mouvant
une mouette crie.

Le train s'arrête.

De petits galets ronds et blancs
remontent le couloir
et s'arrêtent
pour lui chatouiller
les doigts de pied.

Fishes

Without a splash
a fish, the color of mud,
flips into my mind.
He's the flounder I caught for fun
long ago—now hook again

the line burning my hand
as through a string of bubbles
he bursts into a hectic flapping wing
crashing to the sand
his white belly, red with blood.

Now gasping, he stares
and suddenly fishes me.
Dry sand scrapes my back.
A giant hook tears
my mouth.

Les Poissons

Sans éclaboussure
un poisson couleur de boue
saute dans ma tête.
C'est le carrelet que j'ai attrapé pour m'amuser
il y a longtemps—à nouveau piégé

la ligne me brûlant la main
lorsqu'il traverse un collier de bulles
et explose tel une furieuse aile volante
s'écrasant sur le sable
le ventre blanc, rouge de sang.

Suffocant, il me fixe
et soudain me pêche.
Le sable sec m'écorche le dos.
Un hameçon géant
me déchire la bouche.

Sometimes in his Poem

The poet's mother is standing in her doorway
and she is young and smiling and calling his name.
His sister is in the front room
playing the Moonlight Sonata.
His father, outside,
mowing the lawn again.

The poet sits on grass he cannot touch.
There's no mud or trash:
no food wrappers, beer cans or bottle caps.
The air is always blue and perfectly still.
The house, freshly painted white
and vacant.

Quelquefois dans son Poème

La mère du poète se tient sur le pas de la porte.
Elle est jeune, elle sourit, et elle appelle son nom.
Sa sœur est dans le petit salon.
Elle joue la Sonate Au Clair de Lune.
Son père, dehors,
tond le gazon de nouveau.

Le poète s'assoit sur l'herbe qu'il ne peut pas toucher.
Il n'y a pas de boue ou d'ordures:
pas d'emballage, de cannettes de bière ou de capsules.
L'air est toujours bleu et complètement calme.
La maison, fraîchement peinte en blanc
et vide.

Happy Hour

In front of the Riviera Café
a layer of sand
softens the sidewalk.
5 beach umbrellas spread shade
on the metal tables.
Near the curb
a fake lifeguard stand
overlooks 7th Avenue.

I sit with my gin & tonic
waiting for something to happen.
Waves of traffic roll by
or slam to a halt
at the light.

Is that you on the No. 10 bus?
I see the wide door opening
feel the soft tar give
below my feet.

In the bar a piano plays ragtime
the notes splashing
through us.

You're here.
We're at the seashore.

Happy Hour

Devant le Café Riviera
une couche de sable
adoucit le trottoir.
Cinq parasols ombragent
des tables en fer.
Près du bord
une fausse tour de guet
surveille la Septième Avenue.

Je suis là avec mon gin-tonic,
attendant qu'il se passe quelque chose.
Des vagues de voitures roulent
ou freinent brusquement
au feu.

Est-ce toi dans le bus numéro 10?
Je vois la portière qui s'ouvre.
Je sens le goudron céder
sous mon pas.

Dans le bar, le piano joue du ragtime
les notes nous éclaboussent.

Tu es ici.
Nous sommes à la plage.

Undergrowth

At the edge of town, pieces
of dark brown glass from bro-
ken bottles of beer stick
in the mud and weeds, stones
from the tipped-over wall stand
on someone's old box spring, wild
roses poke through worn-smooth
Goodyear Tires, violets climb
from the pock-marked kettle
we threw away.

Sous-Bois

À la sortie de la ville, des éclats
de verre brun : bouteilles de bière brisées
sortent de la terre et des herbes folles,
les pierres du mur écroulé
recouvrent un quelconque sommier,
des rosiers sauvages poussent à travers
des pneus Goodyear usés jusqu'à la corde,
des violettes sortent de la bouilloire percée
que nous avions jetée.

Here? Here at the A & P?

Is that you, Eleanor?
Eleanor, my peach my plum
among the frozen apple pies
in Aisle 7 ?
Stocking up, are we?

And that old fool
fondling melons
from Brazil.
Can that be me?
Impossible.

Ici ? Au Supermarché

C'est bien toi, Eléonore ?
Eléonore, ma pêche, ma prune
parmi les tartes surgelées
au rayon 7.
Alors, on stocke ?

Et ce vieux fou
qui caresse les melons
du Brésil
c'est vraiment moi ?
Impossible.

photo by Bob Cooley

Sanford Fraser has been a student of painting in Paris and a social worker in New York City where he now lives. He has an A.B. degree in literature from Wesleyan University and a Ph.D. degree in art education from New York University. He has been published in *The New York Quarterly, Barrow Street, Chronogram, The New Laurel Review,* and *Turnstile* among others. His chapbook, *14th Street,* appears in The New School Chapbook Series of 1995. In 2007, **Among Strangers I've Known All Life/ Parmi Les Etrangers Que J'ai Connus Toute Ma Vie** was published in a bilingual edition by Tarabuste Editions in France, where he has also published poems in numerous magazines. In 2009, his collection of poems, *Tourist,* was published by NYQ Books.

www.sanfordfraser.com

About NYQ Books™

NYQ Books™ was established in 2009 as an imprint of The New York Quarterly Foundation, Inc. Its mission is to augment the New York Quarterly poetry magazine by providing an additional venue for poets already published in the magazine. A lifelong dream of NYQ's founding editor, William Packard, NYQ Books™ has been made possible by both growing foundation support and new technology that was not available during William Packard's lifetime. We are proud to present these books to you and hope that you will continue to support The New York Quarterly Foundation, Inc. and our poets and that you will enjoy these other titles from NYQ Books™:

Barbara Blatner	*The Still Position*
Amanda J. Bradley	*Hints and Allegations*
rd coleman	*beach tracks*
Joanna Crispi	*Soldier in the Grass*
Ira Joe Fisher	*Songs from an Earlier Century*
Sanford Fraser	*Tourist*
Tony Gloeggler	*The Last Lie*
Ted Jonathan	*Bones & Jokes*
Richard Kostelanetz	*Recircuits*
Iris Lee	*Urban Bird Life*
Kevin Pilkington	*In the Eyes of a Dog*
Jim Reese	*ghost on 3rd*
F. D. Reeve	*The Puzzle Master and Other Poems*
Jackie Sheeler	*Earthquake Came to Harlem*
Jayne Lyn Stahl	*Riding with Destiny*
Shelley Stenhouse	*Impunity*
Tim Suermondt	*Just Beautiful*
Douglas Treem	*Everything so Seriously*
Oren Wagner	*Voluptuous Gloom*
Joe Weil	*The Plumber's Apprentice*
Pui Ying Wong	*Yellow Plum Season*
Fred Yannantuono	*A Boilermaker for the Lady*
Grace Zabriskie	*Poems*

Please visit our website for these and other titles:
www.nyqbooks.org

Sanford Fraser writes about existentialism the way Ernest Hemingway wrote about boxing, you can tell he lived it first. Tourist *is a treatise on memory. It is not for television watchers or John Wayne fans. Like Peter, Paul and Mary used to sing, "Where have all the flowers gone?" I say they went to Sanford Fraser. Through the reconstruction of his memories, he keeps more than flowers alive for us. In essence, he helps us claim back our own memories. A great book.*

—Hal Sirowitz, former poet laureate of Queens, New York

The poetry of the New York poet Sanford Fraser uses images from life to show life. It catches the ephemeral instant to express thirst for the eternal. It is a poetry in which, as in Cummings or François de Cornière…, the insignificant suggests that nothing in life is insignificant. Sanford Fraser snaps pictures that by themselves say the world is what it is: an impure thing. He lets us hear the immensity of solitude—a solitude almost ontological: we appear and we disappear alone. For years, I have attentively followed the poetic development of my friend Sanford Fraser and I can say that he says something essential: social realities are truly the expression of ontological realities because existence gives us every other minute allegories of being and of nothingness. It is sufficient to look. The latest collection of Fraser could only be called Tourist *because it defines the tourist, this passenger, this passer-by, is what he sees. The tourist: a witness who passes.*

—Jalel El Gharbi, Faculty of Letters, University of Manouba, Tunis. He is a critic, an essayist, and a poet.

La poésie de Sanford Fraser, poète new-yorkais, choisit des images de la vie pour dire la vie. Elle se saisit de l'instant éphémère pour dire sa soif d'éternité. C'est une poésie qui, comme chez Cummings ou chez ce poète François de Cornière…, l'anodin insinue que rien n'est anodin dans la vie. Sanford Fraser happe des images qui, par elles-mêmes disent que le monde est ce qu'il est: chose immonde. Il laisse entendre l'immensité de la solitude. Une solitude quasiment ontologique: nous apparaissons et nous disparaissons seuls. Cela fait des années que je suis attentivement le cheminement poétique de mon ami Sanford Fraser et je puis dire qu'il dit quelque chose d'essentiel: les réalités sociales sont plutôt l'expression de réalités ontologiques car l'existence nous offre à chaque instant des allégories de l'être, du néant. Il suffit de regarder. Et le dernier recueil en date de Fraser ne pouvait que s'intituler Tourist *car ce qui définit le touriste, ce passager, ce passant, c'est qu'il voit. Le touriste: un être du regard qui passe.*

—Jalel El Gharbi, La Faculté des Lettres de l'Université de la Manouba, Tunis. Il est critique, poète, essayiste.

Reviews of *Tourist*, 2009

Here, the Outsider speaks. Broken, human, just like the rest of us. But honest, oh so honest. Sanford Fraser has crafted a fine collection. Here he examines the small things and the spaces and people around them. True, perceptive, and evocative throughout.

This is good work.

—Phillip Levine, poetry editor *Chronogram Magazine*

Sanford Fraser's Tourist *is an absolute delight! His suitcase is filled with gems like "Blue Hair," and "Passersby" with their gritty authenticity, and he makes sure to pack a quicksilver moment with stark, fresh imagery that is at once magnanimous and intriguingly out of reach. The temptation to read this book over and over again is overwhelming along with the recognition that this is what poetry is, the senses forever growing up.* Tourist *is a magical work.*

—Jayne Lyn Stahl, author of *Riding with Destiny*

Sanford Fraser is terse, poignant, playful, sly, sharp-tongued, urban & urbane, humane & crafty, all at the same time. Wherever his keen eye turns, a blue-haired girl crossing 14th Street, a crippled woman on a suburban lawn, a raucous motorcycle macho man, an oblivious business man in a European suit, a waitress, a warmonger, a pinup girl, a bum, he sees a poem needing to be painted with words. Often with just a few slim couplets, a score or so of perfect nouns & verbs. But beneath the hard surface of these gems is a greater beauty, an emotional interior of pain, of isolation, of memories & regrets amid the treasured temporary connections of everyday life.

If you visit any of his Tourist *poems ("My Wall," "In Front of the waitress," "Love Song" are among my favorites) you will want to return again and again.*

—Angelo Verga, author of *Praise for What Remains*

www.ingramcontent.com/pod-product-compliance
Lightning Source LLC
LaVergne TN
LVHW051845080426
835512LV00018B/3084